A Library for Juana

THE WORLD OF SOR JUANA INÉS

BY Pat Mora ILLUSTRATED BY Beatriz Vidal

Children's Book Press, an imprint of Lee & Low Books Inc.

New York

Acknowledgments

I wish to express my gratitude to the *Sor Juanistas*,
scholars of Sor Juana, particularly Margaret Sayers Peden.
—P.M.

Originally published by Alfred A. Knopf/Random House, Inc.

Redesign by David and Susan Neuhaus/NeuStudio
Production by The Kids at Our House
The text is set in 14-point Songti
The illustrations are rendered in watercolor and gouache
Manufactured in China by Jade Productions
Printed on paper from responsible sources
10 9 8 7 6 5 4 3 2 1
First Lee & Low Books edition, 2019

Library of Congress Cataloging-in-Publication Data
Names: Mora, Pat, author. | Vidal, Beatriz, illustrator.
Title: A library for Juana: the world of Sor Juana Ines / by Pat Mora;
illustrated by Beatriz Vidal.
Description: First Lee & Low Books edition. | New York: Children's Book Press, 2019.
Identifiers: LCCN 2018046324 | ISBN 9781643790589 (pbk.: alk. paper)
Subjects: LCSH: Juana Ines de la Cruz, Sister, 1651-1695—Juvenile
literature. | Women authors, Mexican—17th century—Biography—Juvenile
literature. | Nuns—Mexico—Biography—Juvenile literature.
Classification: LCC PQ7296.J6 Z6993 2019 | DDC 861/.3 [B]—dc23
LC record available at https://lccn.loc.gov/2018046324

For my book-loving children,
Bill, Libby, and Cissy.
—P.M.

A mis padres,
que me dieron alas y rosas y miel.
—B.V.

"Juana Inés!" called her mother. "What are you doing?" Juana closed the big book. Her grandfather, Abuelo Pedro, was always reading. Here in his house near Mexico City in *Nueva España*, he had stacks of books everywhere. Juana liked to make a nest with his books all around her. She opened them, turning the pages and looking for pictures. She was too little to read, but she wondered what all the words said.

Juana was born many years ago, in 1648. "Why?" was three-year-old Juana's favorite question.

"Why do volcanoes smoke?" Juana asked when she played outside and looked at two mountains puffing white smoke.

"Mamá, why are leaves green?" she asked when she collected wildflowers by the river. Juana liked the soft and thorny roses by her house best. With her fingertip, she stroked their furled petals and touched their prickly thorns. She smelled their sweet redness. Juana even sang rhymes to the roses, "*Rosa hermosa, rosa hermosa.*"

She played with sounds when she skipped down the dirt road, saying, "*Luna, cuna. Bella, estrella.*"

One morning Juana's big sister said, "Juana Inés, I can't play with you today."

"Why?" asked Juana.

"I'm going to learn to read at our neighbor's house," said her sister. "I'm going to read books like Abuelo."

"Me too! I want to go with you!" said Juana Inés. "Mamá, I want to learn to read!"

"But you're too little, Juana Inés," her mother said.

Every day Juana and her mother watched her sister leave for school. One morning when her mother was busy, Juana followed her sister, hiding carefully behind trees and bushes. When the big girls went inside, Juana stood on her tiptoes and peeked in the window. She saw the girls reading and writing.

The next day, Juana again followed her sister to school, but she didn't hide. She walked up to the teacher and said, "*Señora*, I want to read. *Por favor*, will you teach me?"

The big girls all giggled at such a little student, but the teacher looked carefully at Juana. Finally, she said, "Yes, you may come to school, Juana Inés, but you must study and behave."

"I am quiet like a turtle," said Juana.

"First you must learn your letters—A, B, C, D . . . ," said the teacher.

"Why?" asked Juana.

"We make words with letters. Look, r-o-s-a." Juana Inés looked at the letters for rose and saw soft red petals.

At home she wrote her letters again and again. She started reading, and she started writing her rhymes too. "Do you want me to write a song for your birthday, Mamá? I will say you shine like a beautiful star, *una estrella bella,* or maybe that you smile like a pretty rose, *una rosa hermosa.* Yes!"

Mi mamá es una estrella bella.

Mi mamá es una rosa hermosa.

For lunch, Juana Inés liked to chew cheese slowly with warm tortillas.

"Don't eat that cheese, Juana Inés. People who eat cheese aren't very smart. The cheese lumps in their brains," said a friend at school.

That day she said to Mamá and Abuelo, "I don't eat cheese anymore. It's bad for my brain."

Abuelo chuckled. "Who told you that?" he asked.

"My friend," said Juana. "I won't eat cheese, Mamá, because I want to go to Mexico City to study."

"Mexico City!" said her mother.

"My teacher said there is a big university there. It has a library with thousands of books. Imagine!"

"Only boys can go to the university, Juana Inés," said her mother.

The next night, Juana marched in to dinner dressed like a boy. "Juana Inés!" gasped her mother. "What are you doing?"

"I'm practicing so I can go to the university in Mexico City when I'm older. I want to go to their library. I want to study about music and plants and stars. I want to write poems. You know girls are as smart as boys, Mamá."

"Juana Inés, you are stubborn as a rose thorn. For the last time, only men can go to the university," said her mother firmly. "You are a very lucky girl who already knows how to read and write. Girls need to help at home."

"But, Mamá, girls can do more than spin and sew," said Juana. "We can study and prove all we know."

When Juana was about eight, she ran into the house, calling, "Mamá! Look! Look! I wrote the best poem for the contest at church! I won the prize: a book. Now I can start my own library."

Books were Juana's teachers. Month after month she studied Abuelo's books. Over and over again, she said, "*Por favor, Mamá,* please let me go to Mexico City to study." Finally, when Juana was about ten years old, her mother sent her to live with her aunt and uncle in Mexico City.

How exciting it was to arrive in the big city! Juana looked at all the people, she listened to the many languages, and she smiled when she rode by the palace and the university. She wrote poems about all she saw. *"Tía María,"* she said to her aunt, *"tanto que ver. ¿Qué voy a ser?* So much to see. What will I be?"

Since girls could not attend the university, Juana's aunt and uncle hired a tutor to teach her at home. "*Señor,* I hear Latin at church. Will you teach me Latin?" she asked him. Juana soon wanted to learn other languages too. She cared more about her books than about her looks. Tapping her head, she said, "Why decorate the outside of my head if the inside is empty?"

Always curious about everything, Juana Inés bubbled with questions. "How do they build such huge churches? And what languages are those people speaking?" When she saw nuns in their long habits, she asked, "Tía María, what do nuns do? Can they study and read all day in the convents?"

When Juana and her aunt walked by the palace, Juana asked, "Who lives in the palace, and what do they do in there?"

"There are gardens," said her aunt, "and a library. The viceroy and his wife live there. They visit with their guests, and they send letters to the king in Spain. Poets visit, and there are wonderful plays and concerts."

"I want to live there!" said Juana. "I can write plays and songs. *Un canto les canto.* I'll sing them a song. I will study very hard," said Juana Inés, "and then I can write better poems for birthdays and feast days like I write to my family, and, Tía, then I can read in the large library."

Juana did study, and when she was fifteen, her aunt and uncle took her to the palace. "So *you* are the young lady who reads so many books and writes wonderful poems," said the viceroy's wife. "You are beautiful as a rosebud, Juana Inés. Would you like to live here at the palace as a lady-in-waiting?" Juana blushed because of all the people looking at her.

The morning she finally walked into the large palace library, she was once again quiet as a turtle. At last. So many books! A huge room full of treasures. Now she could come every day and touch the many books, slowly read the titles. She read books about calendars and stars, about women in the Bible and in Greek and Roman stories.

Juana wrote plays and songs, and soon many people in the palace heard she liked word games. They came and asked her to write poems and riddles for them. She studied a rose and said, "Look. Its thorns are its prickly royal guards." And she was still curious. "Why does a rose live longer when it's cut, I wonder?" She laughed and teased, "If men learn to cook, they will write a better book."

One day the viceroy said, "Juana Inés, I tell scholars how smart you are, but they don't believe me. I want you to prove it. I've invited forty scholars to come and ask you questions. Members of the court will watch."

"If that is your wish, Señor," said Juana. "My head has always been full of questions. I started reading when I was three so I could find the answers."

"Three?" said the viceroy's wife.

"Yes," Juana said, and laughed. "I followed my big sister to school."

Juana wondered what the forty scholars would ask her. Her head felt full of languages, names, numbers, poetry, and music.

The scholars arrived in their long black robes. They looked very serious. They began to ask Juana difficult questions about triangles, about painting, about famous men, and even about the movement of the planets.

Juana answered every question. When the scholars finished, they nodded. Juana Inés smiled and said, "Yes, girls can do more than spin and sew. We can study and prove all we know." The viceroy's wife hugged her and handed her a beautiful red rose.

Juana liked living at the palace, and she liked her many friends there, but she wanted to keep learning. She needed quiet to think and to write with her quill. She became a nun and changed her name to Sor Juana Inés de la Cruz. She liked the quiet of the convent. She added books to her library until it became one of the largest libraries in the Americas. In her long habit, she prayed and studied and wrote letters, religious songs, plays, and poems. Her friends came to visit her, and she laughed and told them riddles.

"Here, Sor Juana Inés," said her good friends one day, "a book by one of the major poets of the Americas." Sor Juana slowly unwrapped the package. Her name was on the cover! She hugged her book with both hands. That night, Sor Juana added her own book of poems to her treasured library.

Glossary

abuelo: grandfather

bella: beautiful

cuna: crib

de la Cruz: of the Cross

estrella: star

hermosa: pretty

luna: moon

Nueva España: New Spain, the Spanish territories in the New World

por favor: please

rosa: rose

señor: sir

señora: ma'am

sor: sister, used only to refer to nuns

tía: aunt

Author's Note

Poet, defender of women's educational rights, intellectual, playwright, environmentalist, wit. I'm fascinated by the seventeenth-century Mexican author Juana Ramírez de Asbaje, known as Sor (Sister) Juana Inés de la Cruz. We know few facts about this child prodigy, born in the rural village of San Miguel de Nepantla when colonial Mexico was ruled by a viceroy appointed by Spain.

Her words reveal her deep love of knowledge and her inquiring mind. Known for her poems in the Baroque style, which was popular at that time, she also enjoyed painting, playing music, collecting scientific instruments, reading, and studying the thousands of books in her large and famous library. When a plague spread through Mexico, Sor Juana helped to care for the sick nuns in her convent but became ill herself. She died on April 17, 1695.

The image of the proud Mexican Muse and Phoenix of Mexico is printed on Mexican currency. Her words are memorized and recited by children and adults throughout the Spanish-speaking world. Sor Juana: the first great Latin American poet.